GIRL
PAPER
STONE

GIRL PAPER STONE

poems by

Laurie Filipelli

Black
Lawrence
Press

Black
Lawrence
Press
www.blacklawrence.com

Executive Editor: Diane Goettel
Cover Design: Mario Champion
Cover art: Mario Champion
Book Design: Amy Freels

ISBN: 978-1-62557-998-0

Published 2018 by Black Lawrence Press.s
Printed in the United States.

To Confess

Contents

Girl 1
The Road to Mora 2
Why I Can't Make Things Easy 5
Enter Daughter 6
"Another girl cries..." 7
Me, and the Me You Draw 9

tarot for the girl 14

Paper 26
Imaginary Summer 27
Doll 28
Surreal Domestic 31
Wife's Song 32
Missing Scene 33
Me, and the Me I Play 34

tarot for the wife 37

And Then 49
Texas SB 5 50
Garden of Light 52
Our Creation of Feminism 53
Warrior 55
As Seen Through 57
The Key 59
Me, and the Invisible Jury 61

tarot for the me 66

Stone 78

Notes 79
Acknowledgements 81

No, the process of transformation consists almost entirely of decay.

—Rebecca Solnit

Girl

There's the me I am and the me I invent whenever you ask for a story—preferably one with unsolved mischief or golden decisions. Apocryphal me has shenanigans, goofy siblings, backyard sing-alongs, parents placidly saving days. As history goes, we've won. You keep a rock collection like I never did right here near your window. We stare for hours. True, once I flew out onto the roof but never told anyone—just you.

The Road to Mora

Lead-colored drops, glittering sheets. A girl lives in a house of rain. Each day she pours herself from bed, looks at her face, grown heavier. By night circles a swollen floor, slick knobs never turn.

❖

Outside: dry ground and passers lift umbrellas to the sun. She could take this as a hopeful sign instead of an uneven stitch. She gazes through the falling drops, listens to them tick.

❖

To the sky she speaks, I've been so unhappy. Water lifts her. On its woven current, walls collapse. The sky replies: Tell another story about bad decisions. Hair streaming, she sings of slippery places. I am raining she thinks. Thunder closes the bridge.

❖

There's nothing but a coat she doesn't wear. Either too hot or a talisman. Either her weight or her freedom. When snow falls, she feels it. And takes three deep breathes before hefting her coat to the sky; the sky refuses. Tosses it to the river; the coat returns. Two choices, really one in the same: white mules gleaming far ahead, or a coat right here like rain.

❖

From a dark well she reaches. Another story:
two monks have arrived at a house of adobe
in sundrenched shirts, with wine.

Why I Can't Make Things Easy

It was spring and the lilacs were in bloom
near the front porch   it was summer
my father's hand   with its gold band
          and a missing finger
smacked my face   years later
with my brothers   I scraped and scraped
then we painted
and the stairs still crumbled

Enter Daughter

Trying to get the bunny ears right
a pea-sized rock in her pocket   glittering
through a beard of bubbles
                              trying to wink
steady as dust on a ceiling fan
on a jagged stone   cracking open wings
endlessly taping   the tiniest hammock
                    but the sky is
too blue she means gray she means blue
green and the hail of her tears
bigger than sky   her covered ears
words if they existed   who over
this racket of grackles could hear

Another girl cries outside the café

I'm perched

on a landing

seventeen eighteen

hairnet askew

a cowbird

carelessly pecking at fries

twenty-one

twenty- *two*

my father counts

a flutter of wings

behind her eyes what I can't

see

my daughter hides

Nineteen

twenty

a man made taller before he dies

by cowboy boots

a bird in hat
worth two small eggs

catches

in another's nest

small woman

saying please don't

help

my arms

unfreeze

the light

Me, and the Me You Draw

I am only some soup at the side of the road
chilled and thumb-swollen   myself a daughter
below the bridge writing *For a good time call God*

But I have no number   near home just goats
without much pattern: in rain resting
on the neighbor's porch   in sun
the yard to the side of the house
in cold   right here near the hedges
but today I see them any old place   and not at all

First there's summer then I think to scrawl—

(my knees   are round   I can feel
          my arms
                    coming out of my torso   sprouting from
                              my neck   small dots on
                              my face
                              meant to be freckles meant to be bites

my heart
          a balloon   with a snowflake
                    attached   behind me   trees block
                              the actual trees)

I visit my father   on another floor

every day a new face mask   a cascade

of crumbs from passing nurses

Whitman dear Whitman tell me it's luck:

a foldout table with rolled out coins

the thermometer's beep   through a quilt-block of darkness

(to the cemetery hill   my toe-stops   cling
my monkey arms
make motion   lines
unstuffed   from gloves
my hands
let go)

TAROT FOR THE GIRL

Moon

The bigger you spin, the lighter you land. The more space you have to catch a fall. Look up at the brightness: half-smile of gold, half-man of cheese. Dear Rabbit, displace them when you shout. *Make room for me. I'm coming!*

Monkey

Good morning, be happy. You're so near and far from an old woman saving her hotdog bun. A point on the map is a bird in her shell, fur still soft. You open your lips and words pour in. Say barely as verily, who dare correct you? No one's permitted to cut your hair. Let sleep stretch your body as it did in the womb. There's room to swim—feet one way, hands the other.

Pouch

It's true you can wind yourself into existence: the right shade of blue cinching the edges, seashells safe inside. But upended each acorn is bound to tumble. So build a turbine. So grow your lawn well beyond regulation. The city has a code. You have a door.

Wings

I'm sorry. This is not what you think. There are levels attached and feather stretches. Brown Ruffle. Blue Glitter. Gold Orb. T/TH, 3-4. Wives watching in their Pilgrim bonnets, while you bump the glass—mud-smeared and sticky, arms flailing, but you try.

Carousel

The circle repeats but each time something alters. Ostrich among grateful deer. An eyebrow is an eyebrow, even lifted. Roots unbroken, teeth held tightly like commemorative coins—each small Yuri Gagarin, mercifully safe. And beyond, a bag of plastic billows; listen, your hair breaks from its braid.

Snowflake

Thread catching in the ripper makes a terrible sound. But whatever.
You're only loosening time. The beauty of a wish on a melting man.
Little known as an eyelash in these parts, little gem before the rain;
imperfection is a sign you must travel far before coal eyes can see.

Tiara

Glitter for me, queen of our city. Princess of the yard. Show us what all your good can do. In the hall of vaulted minerals with innards of sliced stones glowing, find the heart inside a heart inside a speckled heart, even if it takes forever.

Cave

Light enters the darkness through your sleeping arm. Rest your head, let fingers spill like hair. Each strand opens a door. Running horses. Stone towers. One shard then another then a treasured pot: you will save your village. Trudge back through mud without mistake. The future is a ballad sung in your name.

Wave

Sweet girl, simply comb your hair. Take a bath with the blue fish and a tiny torpedo. Keep counting the molecules you wash from your face, and before you dry off, bask in unknowing. Your skin is your skin was your skin and is growing.

Angel

Don't worry about goodness, simply rise above. You're not as fragile as once was thought. Up here on the rooftop, unafraid to fall, blast your halo around us. Then leave.

Paper

You draw a picture in which I'm your mother, and you're a mermaid. Color seeps into paper made of stone, into fossils beneath our hands. You grip a string that carries us to the stars. For keeping their secret, we are transformed. Back East we measure 55 steps from one end of the whale to the other. All around us stuffed seals and plastic swords. I remember this whale—as big as my world. This house a star we were looking for, a star with a door inside.

Imaginary Summer

To be seven in Texas is a drugstore bikini surfing home on the board of an SUV. Our half of the duplex has dead passion flowers, ankles swollen with harmless venom, pill bugs in a jar. At seven, I stand on a tire swing, back pockets rising with crickets. Grass juts from my hair; new teeth won't uncross. I never get farther than a cul-de-sac, every turn the same.

Doll

She needs a new dress. You take off her clothes
and unplug an arm. Butterflies, glitter.

I find fabric; you fold a seam. She watches
impassive, hair unbraided. As a girl

I smoothed her Polish folk apron, placed her
next to Sacagawea in a flower-print box with

a Madame Alexander stamped *Argentina 571*,
Holly Hobbies with bonnets, unbended knees.

As a girl you find them department-store fresh.
One still has tinsel in her hair.

I never named them. You name this one
after yourself before threading a needle.

(When did you learn?) Temptation. Eyeing
my underbelly, *What would happen,* you ask,

if I sewed me to you? No answer. You go on
like an expert: *We just need a whipstitch.*

A button-hole, a sleeve? I replace the arm,
and imagine myself a reverse Hans Bellmer.

We are in our kitchen. You don't know
the Surrealists, or their suffering mothers.

The perfection of a past viewed through
a doll's navel. Out here in life, Rilke said something

like remembering dolls makes us feel unlovable.
Careful braids, starched lace, my own rag curls

and patent leather used to matter. Our doll
in her new dress and mismatched belt asks

what good have you clung to? Her eyes fall shut.
She's thinking what comes next.

Surreal Domestic

The past as seen through cooking oil
The present leaky fire
The day's first dancing garbage truck
        and leaf-store sidewalk sale
A continent of cupcake stickers
An ocean: teardrop soup
Forget-me-world of angry stairs
The rain as hand soap in my hair
Unnamed: the no one else inside
Five dreams, and one of them is mine

Wife's Song

Starts skygreen as a glow in the chest
cracks like a tree branch, her lips
a deluge of lost notes, plastic fossils
a lone mop tumbling down the street
collides with a dirt bike, a pickup curbed
strains the guardrails to remember a name
tumbles like hail on a tin roof, wails
now a river, now a siren rising
from every direction, shifts and turns
ends and the sun, and the neighbor's trash
lifts like a skirt in the wind

Missing Scene

Umbrella raised against mistakes, I gather
stones and weight the stage. Just out of view

just over land, a painted mountain. Look
beyond—there's Wife cast in a spandex suit.

She's fierce, she's like a tarot card. Let father
grumble his wish to sleep. Let me remember

a car with wings, a bike that pedaled across
the moon. Hilltops before those soldiers came.

My angel playing alto sax. Who offers up
this chance again—someone who isn't dreaming?

Me, and the Me I Play

I am only a chimp in a 3-D mask
                gazing out from a school bus

a monster
                tearing at an airplane wing
                in my pocket   a torn cloud
                                            turning

Come September

Headmistress of this pillbox hat

I lead tours of the attic

here hold this wobbly-headed giraffe

here lift the soft plum of my arm

of my mother's arm

of her mother's arm

Hold my eyes   Little Rabbit

bones flow from the past

like volcanic ash

Now repeat after me:

O snake of fruition

O lying machine

Create your own feather

Count backward from three . . .

TAROT FOR THE WIFE

Lock

The propane grill is first to go, then clothes of joy. Old Elvis delayed on the sagittal plane. A knob stuck like forgotten shoes. Abandon the criminal to her crime. That tunnel: a winter that shut you out. That ladder turns with genetic code, climb carefully, step through.

Balloon

With a pinprick sinking down. How could we forget? Brightest star. Empty heart. How could we forsake you to merciless trees? Label you with our latest slogan? Now that you've uncovered this helium racket, you must make your own heat. See *Wings*.

Hammock

It's hard to get in, harder to get out. Take a womb and its myriad layers. Take a net cast in an ocean of krill. Take the trees and tie yourself to them. When you look up, you'll see the circle framed is sky inside the sky.

Snow

The monk you put on a pedestal was ordering whiskey all the while, then melting his bones into gold. O dear ascetic, who fills his own innards with paper scraps? Lest you forget: it was winter when those cardinals came slow as fog to your dangling feeder, you never saw swallows stuffed in their corpses. Their homes like empty hives.

Labyrinth

You test the water five times a day. You stop to watch the river run and find between your hat and boots a woven beard of graves. Night ten, again you face the shadows but now you have a crooked wand. Iridescent globes floating downstream. What else is there to follow?

Mirror

What but memory makes us stare? Through the past like a hood, through our own gloved fingers. Find a wrinkle, and you'll wish to stitch it over. Find your town, evanescent as a circus, the creek each day stained a different color. No one thought themselves poison, even the mannequin turning away. No beauty surpasses your own.

Gold

Such perfect light begins in pain. For days, sun like a yellow brute scratches the glass. A gift is what you covet so, let go. Let go. Coins are falling from the sky. Unto the Earth. Unto the soil. No barrel here to catch the rain. A flood might fill the reservoir and also cause your home to rot. This feeling tight across the skull, a halo's ugly birth.

Nest

One day you'll simply assess what you've got: a cable sweater drawn from a dumpster, chip from an old board, hair from a comb kept by your mother on her counter for fifty years. You could make snow globes of shaking teeth, but it won't be enough. With or without claw-bottomed slippers, your footprints are destined to become fossils, your ribs an empty cage.

Cape

O musty relic! You've waited long by the museum door, near the elk of gold and the model train. You've waited patient as a glove, to be lifted from the ancient pile, to be worn again. Remembered.

Grackle

Sometimes the gift is to be unpleasant. Squawk then guzzle. Let days like sugar packets spill. If you find your place is on the wire, spread wings with the others to block the sun. This bout is about forgetfulness. A hard freeze in a rusty cage. The rosemary remains and a little gnome. A hula hoop. That ladder.

And Then

Outside the theater my yellow-dressed girl—cowbird shitting straight at you. Everything turns white: missing notes memory podium dream. Bedside the next morning, you rightly upbraid me. I squeeze myself into a smaller self, tumble onto the floor, wake up.

Texas SB 5

We're trying to grow something besides shrunken tomatoes. You want flowers, California-like, a rotunda of dahlia. It all makes me teary: the chanting, the Senators reading from scripts. And here at the nursery, a skinny pants guy pointing out plumbago, perfect blue. It needs no rain, or cool air, somehow even sun. The neighbor kid busy building fairy trenches. Me in dress sandals. You in sparkly shoes. We kick until the plant breaks free, then I dump all the compost as if to prove something. Limestone you break with a plastic gavel. I'm having nightmares, pre-dinosaur style. Officers wave gingko, put plugs in their ears. Awake we've gone past dahlia gardens to the carousel: First the blue horse, then the dolphin, then the giant rabbit.

It's good to be cold, good to watch you spinning steadily past. My mom stands behind and I think I won't always know my place, right here in the middle. But also I think of Phoebe Caulfield. Even without your bouquet at the airport, the TSA guy orders you to stop. And waves me forward. *What the fuck,* I think, *She's only four.* Carousel gone, too late I turn. You run into my arms. You still want flowers. We don't know yet we'll find plumbago, and the bill will pass. Because you were frightened, I should go back. He's just some guy, just some guy, but I say nothing.

Garden of Light

I am assigned the job of angel wrangler. They all complain in a tiny house lit by one lantern—who gets which robe, how to sit with wings—and shove more cookies in their mouths. Accidentally, one knocks out the flame. I hold a flashlight.

On request watch them shape shadows into dogs. There's only a half bag of pretzels left. When the signal comes, they bustle out and down the path, I mouth *walk slowly* to no avail, and think never again.

Our Creation of Feminism

In the beginning, an endless tiara,
those tissue box princesses, as much

as I hated your tippy toe dance
was hard not to love. What I'd wanted

came back: that dump truck, that crane.
That joke about six and its fear of seven?

Let us say on day two you bore your claws,
drew our portrait as a family living in caves.

(In the next booth Wife growls
and orders more beer.)

Then came day three. In dry erase crayon
scrawled on our mirror—*Let the net throw stones.*

Long ago I longed for a wax mustache
to be Cather playing Beauty's merchant father.

The past tears like a leotard, like handmade
tickets to Dancing Queen. So gladly we stomped

on that old parade. Day four brought us poster board.
Wrenching rusty wheels off on afternoon five,

the neighbor's wife won the prettiest gun.
Day six? Its foam box stored an agate necklace.

Day seven came and went.

Warrior

Sleep my stupid last-year
person, stooping to pick up

whatever falls (so much
with scraps of fever building

a time machine—old cane,
Christmas needles). Awake

a chain hooks my Achilles.
The yard is small, the moon

still on the neighbors' side.
We are playing Orpheo

Looks Back. You hand me
fishtails, shimmering clues.

A guardhouse birded by
a porcelain cat. A trash bag

taking flight. When I step
on a scale, its metal arm

pushes me shorter. Between
one and ten, this pain

is a three which means
I am free to go home.

As Seen Through

A guard fetches water for a Chihuahua
and I learn my father is still alive.

Pull the spit from my eye; it is not contagious.
The president, too, had teenaged fears.

Dad, tell us again—

the whale's veins are so wide we could swim
to her heart, as big as a car. We could lift

a small plane with the span of her tail.

Here was a growth, a strange sea coral,
beautiful and benign. When cut

it shimmered from my breast.
Then my voice decayed and above me

my wings—tissue paper and dust—
streamered through spokes of a ceiling fan.

The nurse's eyes too blue, my skin
wrinkled balloons. From the center of Antarctica

my father shouts, "This—

is the loneliest place on Earth." And now
his tousled hair flies.

The Key

lives in a drawer at the edge of freedom
or sticks
like a pushpin in the last hometown
tied with green ribbon
on a wobbly shelf
making do with a small cat
and smaller hope

left aloft on a car roof it's a cup half full
clanking down to the bridge
spilling bright
on the waves

(pull back

pull further)

and darkness

opens

Me, and the Invisible Jury

Woodpeckers carve trunks to sticky lace

but I am no bird

                                        eating straw boots

I learn   once more to love my mother

I learn not to laugh when the wife on TV

hands over the twins

                                        but my sides are splitting

In chalk I write *Time is running out*
          and time runs out as I write—
a thought-grain dangling   an angry god

          (wind   the sky   known blue
                    the slope
                              though slippery   still burns)

Fiery pit   political slop
I've nailed the division
                    but not the source
betrayal was only an empty bucket
                    remembering itself as a beautiful vase

(Father's hands were swollen
        his hands were cold
                but his ring was not in the bin of rice
        in a lot full of pebbles
                his ring was a stone
                        cracked open to reveal
                                a butterfly's wing)

Keep a shadow box as my defense
                    a well-pressed silence
keep a heart
                    unbroken and the birds won't come
keep that flag   it's my body
that needs to unfurl

Gap-toothed   I'll sing

if you raise your martini   if it pleases the jury

I'll spit out a toast:

to the daughters above

ripping seams from the sky

to the wives who shovel trucks into snow—

let's unfold our cots   we are here

TAROT FOR THE ME

Dear Laurie

I hear you yelling alone in the car, gripping until your head goes numb. I see you pacing until you fall. The moon grows, a mushroom above your yard. A spider wraps its bee in silk. Everyday the floor chips, and then there's a pattern like an eagle's head, some sheep.

Dear Laurie

Your father was anxious like his mother before him. In one story he went MIA, and she bounced a baby on his bed for luck. His father, hit by a city bus, or hit by the mob. Uncertainty is uncertain like that. The bullet goes clean through.

Dear Laurie

That pounding in your ears? It's the miniature gavel called your heart. No one wants to hear your dishwater defense. The alarm clock evidence. Your sentences, always incomplete. The jury has hung itself to dry with a tiny bike and a pillbox hat. See, the moon's still growing.

Dear Laurie

Perhaps you are the daughter you keep forgetting. Days old and lifted from the crib, left out on the steps, or somewhere among a houseful of friends no one happens to know. Ask the mom in the courtyard when she hands you a joint. Ask her where you've gone.

Dear Laurie

Keep talking until you feel understood but stay quiet in the morning kitchen, unnaturally cluttered with lunches. Who knows why the stone ape was led astray? Beyond the waterfall lay immortality, just one page in his crumpled hand.

Dear Laurie

When you back up the car and make a U-turn, your vision will blur to a field of gray. Take a deep breath, this happens all the time. She's not in the backseat. She's wherever you left her. When the power fails, hold your mother's hand. Find yourself on a small plane looking down. There's the mythic city, gold-plated like a tidal wave. The place you wish you'd gone.

Dear Laurie

Practice writing your name with third-grade precision and I guarantee you'll feel loved. As a girl when you hid, the instructions were clear: you must cover your head. Now the key is silence, impenetrable silence. Keep looping your L's. Teach your daughter the lost art of saving herself. It's easy as an embroidery hoop. Just stitch every color inside.

Dear Laurie

I will now find something for you to take with you, a golden orb beyond the billowing smoke, a talisman lost through a hole in the sky, a shotgun to the head. Use it to unmake hospital corners, find your father waving monkey arms: Look at me, I can move. Look, I'm free!

Dear Laurie

Revert after all to small noble acts. For example, save a heritage tree.

Dear Laurie

Because you spoke to a stone you need a steroid shot, and you still want to speak to another. The professor can't help but your daughter can climb above the stage, loosen ropes from rafters, your failure lodged in her teeth. The clock ticks away, you wish for a toothbrush. The bristling understood.

Stone

Take my hand I am ready to drop these vines,
said the god of the garden with feathers
singed. Chest lifted, I'm pelting back the rain
and the paper dragon burns. What is left but
past beneath the past, a floodgate lowered,
and me no longer a tender river. I follow each
current. A girl of silt concentrates so hard she
becomes a wife. Almost swept away, this dust
now orbits   in a ring of tiny light.

Notes

P. 2 The title of the poem "The Road to Mora" (as well as the rain, mules, and monks) draws from Book 2, Chapter 2 in Willa Cather's *Death Comes for the Archbishop.*

P. 19 Yuri Gagarin, referenced in the "Carousel" section of *Tarot for the Girl*, was a Russian-Soviet pilot and cosmonaut. In 1961, he became the first person to journey into outer space.

P. 28 Hans Bellmer, referenced in "Doll," was a German photographer, sculptor, printmaker, and writer. When the Nazis gained power in 1933, Bellmer gave up all work that might be deemed useful to the State and began building a life-size doll that could be assembled and reassembled like a machine. Bellmer is most famous for his two cycles of controversial photographs of the posed doll, which were taken between 1933 and 1939.

P. 50 Texas Senate Bill 5 (or Texas SB 5), discussed during the First Special Session of the Eighty-third Texas Legislature, is a list of measures that restrict abortion access. The bill was signed into law by Gov. Rick Perry in 2013, and declared unconstitutional by the United States Supreme Court two years later. At the time of publication, women in Texas continue to struggle for their right to obtain abortions and adequate healthcare.

P. 53 "Our Creation of Feminism" makes reference to Willa Cather's childhood. In 1888 she donned a suit, top hat, and wax mustache to play Beauty's merchant father in a production of *Beauty and the Beast* at the Red Cloud Opera House.

Acknowledgements

Thanks to editors at the journals and magazines where the following poems were previously published: "Warrior" *Superstition Review* (16); "Me, and the Me You Draw" *Xavier Review* (34.1); "Girl" published as "Stone" *BOAAT* (5); "Another girl cries..." as "A woman cries outside the café" *So and So Magazine* (8); "The Road to Mora" and "Garden of Light" *The Pinch* (34.2); "Wife's Song" *Salamander* (38); "Texas SB 5" *apt literary magazine* (Summer 2014); "Surreal Domestic" *Redheaded Stephchild* (Spring 2014).

Thanks to Mario Champion for the book cover photograph and design.

Thanks to Austin arts supporters Carla McElhaney at *Revel* and Susan Post at *Book Woman* for encouraging colllaboration through their inspiring events. And to Chris Tonelli for welcoming me as part of the *So and So Poetry Series* in Raleigh, N. Carolina.

Thanks to Yaddo for providing me with the space, time, courage and magic without which this book would not have been completed.

Thanks to Laurie Saurborn, Irena Smith, and Vivé Griffith for their cheerleading, insight, and editorial feedback. To Mario Champion for loving my poetry, and me. And to Eliana for being a girl, an artist, a thinker, a helper—the best part of my story.

Laurie Filipelli is the author of *Elseplace* (Brooklyn Arts Press, 2013) and *Girl Paper Stone* (Black Lawrence Press, 2018). Her essays and poems have appeared at *apt magazine*, *The Rumpus*, *Salamander*, *Superstition Review* and elsewhere. She is the recipient of a Yaddo fellowship and lives in Austin where she provides coaching and editing services through her business, Mighty Writing.